contemporary british jewellery
unclasped

contemporary british jewellery

unclasped

Derren Gilhooley   Afterword by Simon Costin

Edited by Alexandra Bradley & Gavin Fernandes

contents

unclasped

by Derren Gilhooley

Like a simple wedding band torn from the finger in rage or despair and cast away, contemporary British jewellery is realising a greater potential for significance in being rent from its traditional position as glamorous accessory and investment heirloom and thrust into new contexts. Jewellery, in its popular forms of gold, strings of pearls or even the beguiling tourist extravagance that is the Crown Jewels, is almost too narrow a term for the work of a new generation of artisans, artists and designers working on the adornment of the body. Issues ranging from communication and nostalgia, to millennial anxiety and historicism, are inherent in their works: objects that advance metaphysical propositions as they clasp the throat, articulate the fingers or illuminate the mouth.

Popular jewellery design, typified by the product of high street chains and high fashion design houses, is dictated by the expedients of mass production and conspicuous consumption. Admittedly, it is misleading to talk about jewellery design as if it is a single entity. To deny difference in the popular, is to ignore the safety pins of punk, multi-ethnic influences, futuristic plastic and perspex, vogues for antique and costume jewellery,

found objects and surrealism; all of which have been themes in fashion jewellery of recent decades. But in much popular jewellery, ideas and innovation are discarded in deference to market forces. Sentimentality, prettiness and garish display have been the design criteria responsible for banal gift items that appreciate only in meaninglessness. At the level of high fashion, design houses produce increasingly self referential bagatelles, using linked initials and brand acronyms that speak only to fashion label initiates, and ultimately threaten to impoverish the language of adornment.

Contemporary jewellery designers now working in Britain, are restoring and expanding this vocabulary. From the conceptualist Naomi Filmer to the intuitive Mike Turner, using non-Western, non-twentieth century sensibilities, and elements of other visual practices, the possibilities for making meaning with body adornments are being rediscovered. The results are a new strain of decorative objects that force a reconsideration of where they belong.

With the elevation of fashion catwalk shows to a kind of costume theatre (vital in bringing media attention to less commercial designer names), styling and accessorising have increased in importance. Many of the most striking and provocative images in recent British fashion, from movie matinee vampire teeth at Hussein Chalayan to a flooded catwalk at Alexander McQueen, have resulted from collaborations between fashion designers and jewellery designers, who are literate across a broad visual culture. Rather than stultify creativity with self consciousness, their presence appears to have had the opposite effect, resulting in images that are ever more extraordinary.

Like all art objects, jewellery has always had the power to exceed its empirical worth with symbolic value. Georges Bataille uses a diamond ring to illustrate what he describes as the irrational economy, where spiritual value exceeds use value. Tutankhamun's burial cache, a Cardinal's ring, a monarch's orb, the lover's keepsake, Elizabeth Taylor's Krupp diamond: all are examples of the capacity for finely worked precious stones and metals to transcend their form, becoming magnified in the realm of the imagination.

Exploration of this capacity for transcendence, dormant in even the most prosaic wedding band, was famously resumed by jewellery designer and creative director of catwalk shows for Alexander McQueen and Givenchy, Simon Costin. In a headline grabbing moment of 1988, an exhibition of his work, including the incubus necklace which incorporated sperm filled vials, caused outrage and eventual police intervention. Costin's real achievement was to make jewellery mean, in ways that could create disturbances (by shocking, provoking and offending) in the wider culture.

The orthodoxies of banal modern jewellery are challenged by New Age designer Mike Turner, with works that return to the possible origins of jewellery, in ritual objects. He unites Celtic tribalism and surreal bodily alienation, in richly patinated pieces that evoke natural and technological forms. Discarding prettiness, Turner strips away jewellery's tinselly qualities, to produce adornments for the modern pagan. They are designed for, or at least suggestive of, a proudly subcultural, customised body. Like Amazon Indian lip plates, Maori tattooing, and the neck rings of some African tribes, these objects cannot easily be removed without leaving a residual trace. They are permanent indicators of individuality, initiation into, and adherence to a marginal way of life and subcultural belonging.

Like the New Flesh nightmares of David Cronenberg and the Japanese Tetsuo films, Turner's collisions of the organic and metallic are an account of the tensions between technological and natural bodies. Startlingly visceral glass eyes and false dentures echo the disturbing imagery of illustrator H.R. Geiger repeating his violent and sexual effects. In Turner's work, a lebrett puncturing the face, nipples or genitals is ritualised and made meaningful through the act of wearing.

The tribal construction of violence, pain and sex, as rite of passage or initiation, is to be found throughout fashion adornment. Chinese foot binding and the wearing of body distorting stilletto shoes for erotic purposes, are just two examples of fashion's inherent sexual violence. Violence is implicit in jewellery's very mechanisms of fastening, piercing, clasping and buckling, but they are often disguised with a floral motif or other abstract design. Sexuality is ever present, not merely with jewellery functioning as a prism to focus nebulous sexual allure, but in the penetration of pin into cloth, the glimmer of ring through navel, the coupling mechanisms of a clasp or the genital display of vegetable and flower forms. As if responding to the increasingly visible subcultural practices of tattooing, branding and piercing, contemporary jewellery designers are making the implicit explicit, with work that openly references violence and sexuality as indicators of belonging to specific taste cultures.

Sexual violence in fashion is typically filtered through the gauze of glamour, but the work of the most visible British fashion designers of recent years, has foregrounded it in an unmediated way. This mirrors punk fashion, where the impulse to use the body as a tool for destructive and procreative acts, and the desire to repel and provoke with dress, collided. Punk's parading of bondage and fetish wear in public spaces transgressed the proprieties of a society that had previously restricted sexuality in fashion to coded forms; uniforms and aristocratic riding clothes and the prurient scenarios of the brothel and the suburban boudoir. Punk flaunted these secrecies on the urban street, in broad daylight. It flashed confusing signals, both liberating and restraining, assaulting coherent identity itself.

Where tribal imperatives are a lesser consideration, the sexual violence of fashion jewellery (pleasure in and for its own sake) can be figurative or abstract in form. The work of Sean Leane is both. His crown of thorns and barbed wire pieces, recall the crucifixion narrative of pain when worn on the brow, or the distressed eroticism of impenetrable forests that grow around fairytale castles, when spiralled around the arm. In these story-telling works Leane conflates religion and superstition.

Less baroque, are the minimal silver head-dresses that appear to slice through the skull or jut from the throat in elegantly menacing needle points. Enlarged and elongated, the image of the penetrative fastening pin becomes an adornment in itself, making the implicitly violent openly threatening. Religion is again evoked in this series, by a slender gem studded halo that encircles the head, irreverently turning the mark of canonisation into a chic adornment.

Blades, claws and knives bristle from the work of Sarah Harmarnee. Fantasy violence, fairy tale evil and piratical ruthlessness are evoked by unyielding snaffle barred necklaces, talon nail extensions, elbow horns and dagger rings fashioned in silver, leather and horn. Shanks of hair provide both a dashing touch and a morbid reference to scalping. An impulse to master and be mastered is implicit in her borrowings from equestrian bridal tack. Street gang violence with a musketeer twist is evoked by baroquely decorated modern adaptations of the stilleto and Bowie knife, akin to the finely worked guns brandished by rival Montagues and Capulets in Baz Luhrman's film William Shakespeare's Romeo and Juliet. The suggestion is that for modern life you need not only to be armed, but to be armed exquisitely.

The subtlety of voguish sadism is taken to extremes in the quill, leather and velvet constructions of milliner and jewellery designer Dai Rees. His very choice of materials evoke the boudoir cruelties of The Marquis De Sade (whose novel Justine is an account of a woman's forced introduction to sado-masochism), where pricking, constraining, pinching and tickling are used for torture and exquisite pleasure. Thorny quill head pieces define the space around the head and divide the face; denuded feathers play about it; velvet masks obscure it and a leather neck corset fixes it rigidly, becoming supple and comfortable with repeated wear. Rees' manipulation of turkey quills: stripping, sanding and covering in glitter, paint, flock and velvet, mirrors the over embellishment of high fashion.

Erik Halley similarly references the feather boas and collars of cinema icons like Dietrich, through the shaping and organisation of plumes into chokers and bracelets; giving a contemporary edge to the sexual signifiers of silver-screen sophistry and cinema vamp imagery. Halley's nostalgic yet elegant repertoire of pieces are rendered in diaphonous bejewelled materials, akin to those used to furnish the wardrobes of Cecil B. de Mille's harem slaves; evoking the decadent glamour of early Hollywood.

Precision violence, inherent in the instruments of invasive surgery (stirrups, scapula and scalpel) and the formal sexuality of machinery, insects and flowers, are themes of the highly articulated work of Mark Woods. His technical training as a ship builder underpins the making of jewellery where ball and socket joints, screws, hinges and nipples, are fetishistically fashioned in clinical silver and phenolic plastic (the material of snooker balls). A psychoanalytical critique finds copious nipples, teats, genitals and couplings that would provide useful material for a thesis on the sexuality of engineered joints.

Wood's jewellery reflects the Surrealist's obsession with the articulated and dismembered human body, from the jointed obscenity of Hans Belmer's Doll sculptures of 1936 to Kurt Seligman's Ultra-Furniture of 1938. The streamlined forms of Art Deco accessories and domestic appliances and the exquisitely morbid, hyper-real dragon-

fly brooches of Lalique, fashionable early in this century, are referenced in Wood's gyrating, trembling pieces.

Bodily issues of another kind, those of touch and communication, are explored in the work of the late Nicole Gratiot Stöber. The erotics of machined surfaces and smooth shapes are capitalised on in pieces designed to light up from within when touched and held. Palm sized pebbles of wood and steel glow reciprocally when caressed. A slender metal baton illuminates only when held at both ends, in the act of being passed from one person to another. Stöber's work encourages an interactivity at odds with much jewellery designed to be admired from a distance. Stöber privileges contact over scopophilia. The body responds to the jewellery and the jewellery responds to the body. This symbiosis is typified by a neck piece with contacts in the shape of golden rose thorns. When placed against the skin a circuit is completed, triggering a pulse of light that travels the circumference of the loop. The light fades gradually when the contact is broken. Stöber's work regards technology benignly, as a medium for communication and self expression. Transmitters and information interfaces operate without male gendered buttons. Switches and probes; clasps, sockets, chains and piercings are noticeably absent in works that by-pass the sadistic baggage of jewellery and further blur the distinction between decorative and artistically autonomous objects.

Ironic references to the technological promises of the past and yesterday's visions of the future, can be found in the retro-chic perspex and plastic jewellery of Janice Taylor. Utopianism features humorously in rings, bracelets and necklaces derived from the wholesome and hygenic forms and materials of twentieth century suburban modernism and sixties futuristic funkiness. Sharp, minimal shapes cut from industrial cast-offs in colourful perspex, reflects the cool colour-field painters such as Ellsworth Kelly and theatre set designs of the Twentieth Century. In keeping with an optimistic view of modernity, a wipe-clean convenience, inflatability and a brighter tomorrow, Taylor reconfigures 40s bakelite influenced pieces into simple, clean cut contemporary shapes.

Lara Bohinc, another futuristic designer, makes cartoonish use of the forms of information technology; tiaras bristle with antennae, head dresses incorporate headphones and microphones. Necklaces trace the lines of flightpath patterns or a chiffon scarf caught in the breeze, and chokers carry cryptic phrases embossed on their surfaces. The objects do not function electronically, but they anticipate a world in which individuals will always be connected to the information super-highway; when body adornments will be smart.

The work of Naomi Filmer comments ironically on the human/machine symbiosis. A head piece, part of a series produced in collaboration with Hussein Chalayan, which echoes a telephone receptionist's headset, plugs both the ear and the mouth, playing with the metaphor of technology imperilling communication. Negatives are a recurrent theme of these pieces, such as mouth bars which hold the mouth open or LEDs that illuminate and accentuate the mouth's void. Filmer discovers new spaces on the body to adorn, with objects designed to nestle in the negative spaces between fingers, teeth and the folds of the ear. In isolation, they are baffling but beautiful, resembling the biomorphic forms in dreamscape paintings by Salvador Dali and Yves Tanguy. When returned to the individual body on which they

were formed and to whom they are fitted, these pieces make sense.

It is tempting to draw comparisons between Filmer and the artist Rachel Whiteread, who casts the spaces around objects such as the void underneath a chair, and even the inside space of an entire Victorian house. Whereas Whiteread's work is haunted by a sense of loss and a comment on the domestic material culture with which we live, Filmer's pieces explore a more surreal vein, the functional and dysfunctional body and its manmade technological extensions.

Filmer's interest in an irregular body reflects a trope of current British fashion. To varying degrees British fashion repudiates the international aesthetic of bodily perfection, typified by Calvin Klein and Giorgio Armani; preferring the ideal of a more characterised beauty, exemplified by models such as Stella Tennant and Karen Elson, aided by the documentary style of fashion photography. Paradoxically, this very individualism and edginess, is now becoming a homogenous look.

The exchange between fine art and adornment is strongly apparent in the work of identical twins Emma and Jane Hauldren, (H2 Design). Their exquisitely finished silver objects (they describe themselves as contemporary silversmiths) can be worn, carried or experienced in exhibition and installation contexts. Largely celebratory of technology and club culture, they produce hip flasks for psycho-active drinks, modelled on body parts. Their rings replace the traditional gemstone or diamond with a capsule for a life extension pill. Twin-hood, separation and longing are explored in other works, including a double stomach flask for sharing amniotic fluids, and a breathing cylinder in which mouths and lungs are united. Their recent experimentation with virtual reality headsets reflects their interest in the altered states of club and drug culture and new ways of experiencing both the 'real' and virtual world. A tradition of jewellery as a facilitator of introspection and contemplation is also accessed by the virtual headset. This time however, the inner life of vanity or votive intention, is supplanted by a cyber-spatial environment. Comparison with the fine artist twins, Jane and Louise Wilson, is inevitable. Their work is similarly concerned with twin-hood and the reproduction of their experiences in dreamscapes (large scale cibachromes in which they reconstruct shared experiences of altered consciousness). By presenting autonomous objects as installation with sound, filmed images and instructions, the work has functions beyond those of mere fashion or adornment. Their use of intestine-like rubber and metal body casting provokes comparison with the work of artists Kiki Smith, Helen Chadwick and Cathy de Monchaux, but their celebratory agenda precludes the abject body. The conflation of self and technology through use of objects, video and interactivity is closer to the practice of an artist such as Georgina Starr, whose works, Getting to Know You and Making Junior, re-present her experiences through video, CD Rom and collections of found objects. Despite the avowed optimism in their work, marooned mouths and artificial umbilici are sudden reminders of the dislocation and alienation of the body and its functions.

Simon Costin and Dai Rees both create a theatrical and narrative strand in their work. They plunder widely different sources such as popular culture, folklore and ethnicity. A similar eclecticism also drives the work of Lars Sture and Laurent Rivaud. Both represent an intelligent approach to the cultural and ethnic piracy that forms the backbone of London's street style and designer fashion.

It is inevitable that Rivaud, jewellery designer for Vivienne Westwood, should be well versed in the use of bricollage. Using a diversity of found objects and traditional jewellery materials he produces elaborate and suggestive objects to articulate the narratives of Westwood's themed collections. The tradition of keepsake and relics in which fragmentary remains become the focus for displaced desires, are referenced in Rivaud's designs which incorporate bone, hair, precious metals and totemic motifs such as skull and crossbones or sea serpents. The configuration of fetish objects becomes a portrait of a protagonist in the collection's narrative. Making an object yield its story is a founding principal of archaeology and art history; the past is explained by its surviving objects. In geology the past is explained through its mineral remains, but Rivaud confounds any methodologies, in pieces that configure minerals into exquisite flower ornaments. Rivaud's postmodern technique of collage playfully rearranges the past regardless of hierarchies and chronologies, to revitalise old narratives and generate new ones.

Where Rivaud gleefully explores Western historicism, Sture accesses global culture. In recent work he makes reference to ethnic jewellery with intricate beaded works for the hands and arms and chunkier chain link bracelets and chokers, resembling refined versions of ostentatious hip hop and bhangra jewellery. A western silversmith working with these influences is vulnerable to accusations of ethnic piracy, but fashion has always used ethnicity as a source of ideas. Paul Poiret plundered the harem.

Yves-Saint Laurent's collections were virtual travelogues of Africa, India, China and Russia. In the eighties and nineties, fashion designers Jean Paul Gaultier and Dries Van Noten, amongst others, have both variously explored the theme of orientalism. In Western culture and fashion, the East has always been a place of the Id and the imagination; where other lives can be lived and other selves explored. Ethnic piracy is an ingrained part of fashion's will to masquerade.

Sture is part of a post-colonial culture, and his work combines ethnic and surrealist elements, to produce objects that readily absorb displaced desires. The use of hair and beading in some pieces recalls the sculpture of Meret Oppenheim and also perhaps the traditions of voodoo magic. In a city as multi-cultural as London, Sture's work is autobiographical; a reflection of what is seen on the streets through which the designer passes daily.

The current interest in British visual and popular culture worldwide, and a resurgence in London's fortunes as a fashion city, has attracted many epithets declaring the capital to be the groundspring of cool and creativity. The maturation of a post-Pop art school generation, influential London colleges such as Central St. Martins and The Royal College of Art, pre-millennial hysteria, a vigorous club culture and a return to the swinging attitudes of the sixties are variously credited with the renaissance. Some of the designers discussed here are not British born, but all make contact with Britain and London at some point, be it through training or collaboration. Like cultural centres that have flourished in the past, London is a meeting place of currents and counter currents, enriched by a diverse

racial, cultural and philosophical mix. British fashion also benefits from its streetstyle, which is not overshadowed by a commercial fashion establishment to the same extent as in other cities. In jewellery design, a raw and argumentative edge distinguishes contemporary British work from the bourgeois Paris style, the business-woman look of New York, and the self referential glamour of Milan. Jewellery has always strayed beyond the confines of adornment.

From the funerary objects of ancient cultures to the wearable reliquaries of Catholicism, jewellery has been invested with considerable power. The images of the lover sliding a ring onto the beloved's finger, and of the husband approaching the wife from behind, to drape a chain around her neck, graphically reinforce the themes of desire, obsession and possession inherent in human relations. Folk and fairytales are haunted by sleeping draughts in rings, poisoned hair-combs and strangling necklaces; these are inevitably carried, via the child's imagination, into the adult psyche. Psychoanalytical studies of the meaning of jewellery, such as Freud's case study of Dora (in which a young woman's recurring dream featuring her imperilled jewellery box, is interpreted as a playing out of her sexual anxieties), have found items of jewellery to be potent subconscious ciphers.

The excitement of contemporary British jewellery design is the result of the designer's willingness to take advantage of this capacity to command the imagination at all levels. As long as they continue to unpack the baggage that accumulates around all bodies of designed objects, the production of new and startling work, and the charting of new territories in bodily adornment, is assured.

Erik *Halley*

Janice Taylor

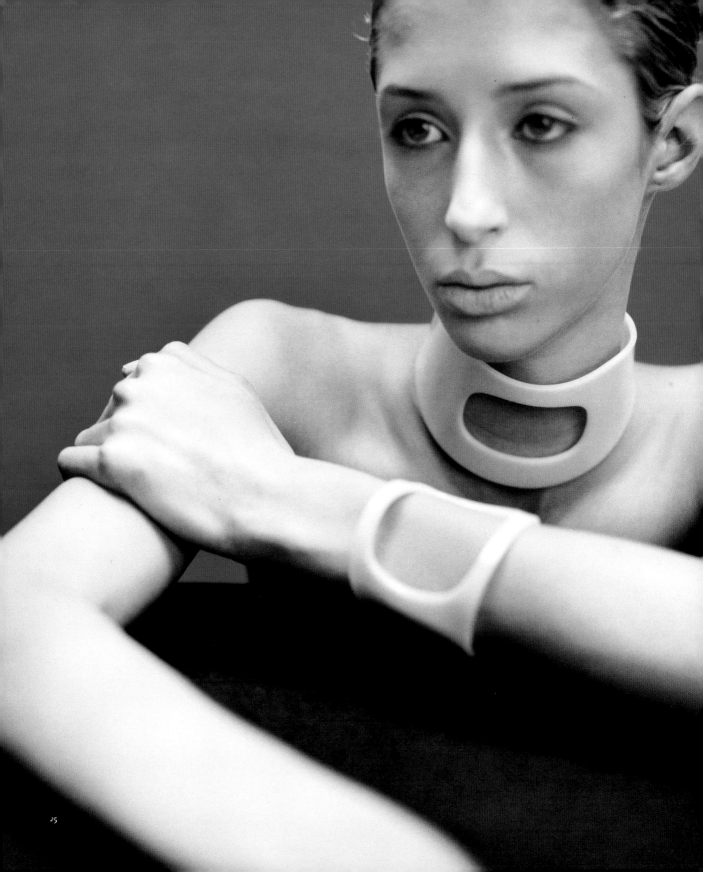

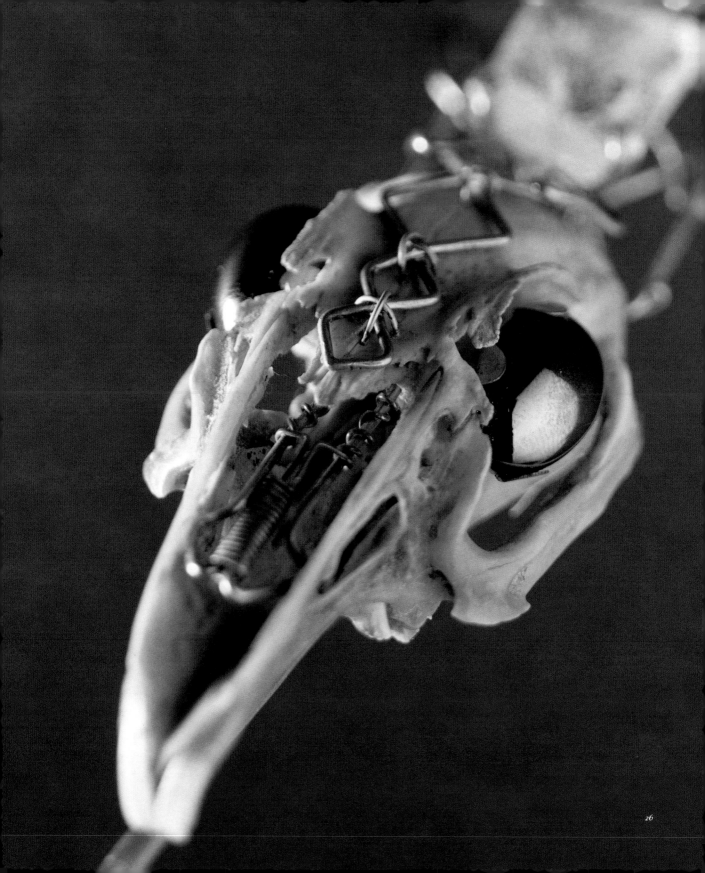

Simon Costin

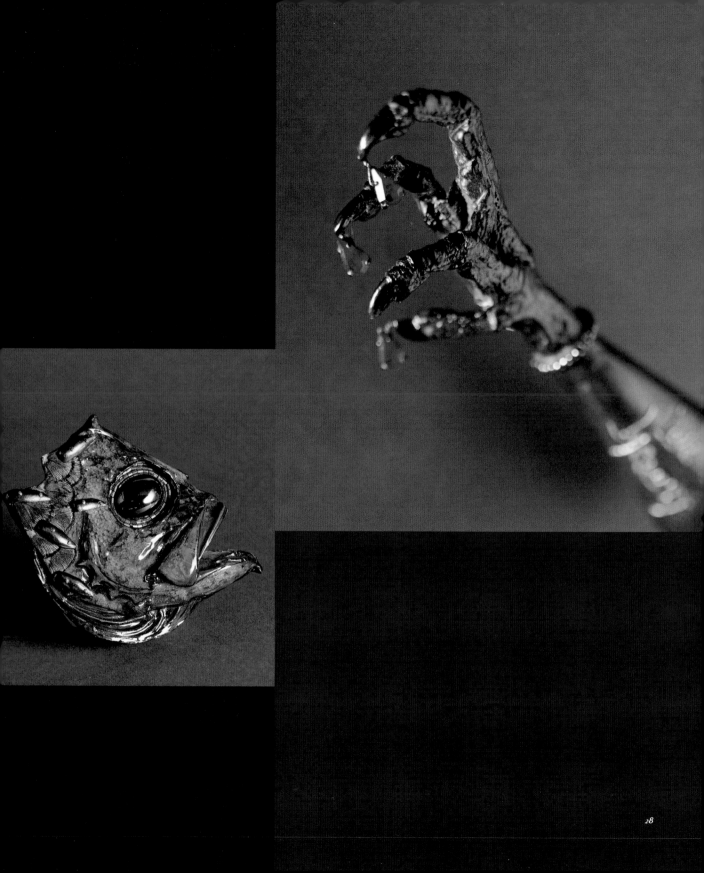

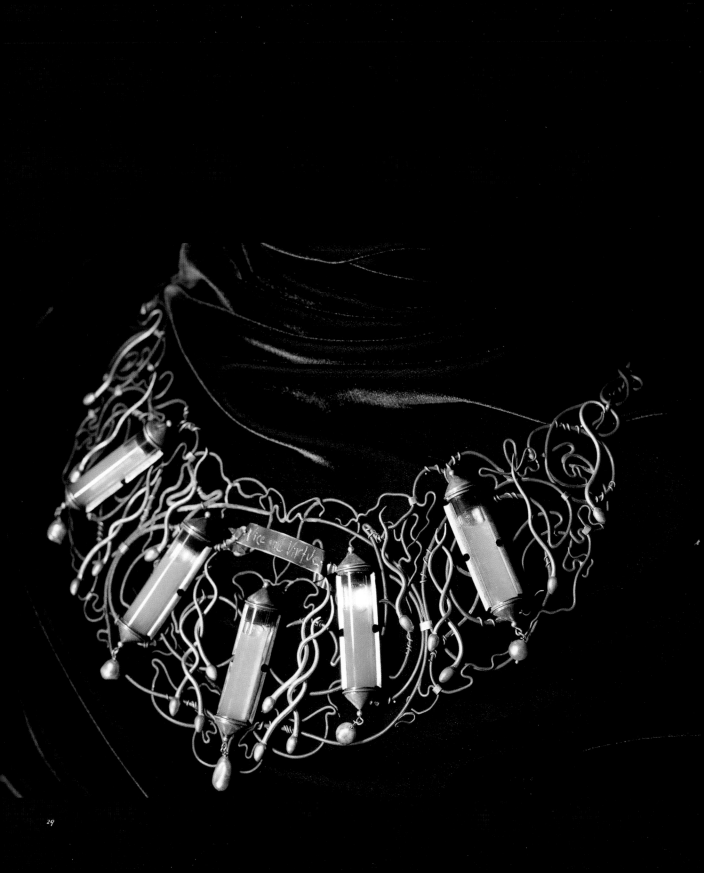

Scott Wilson

Naomi *Filmer*

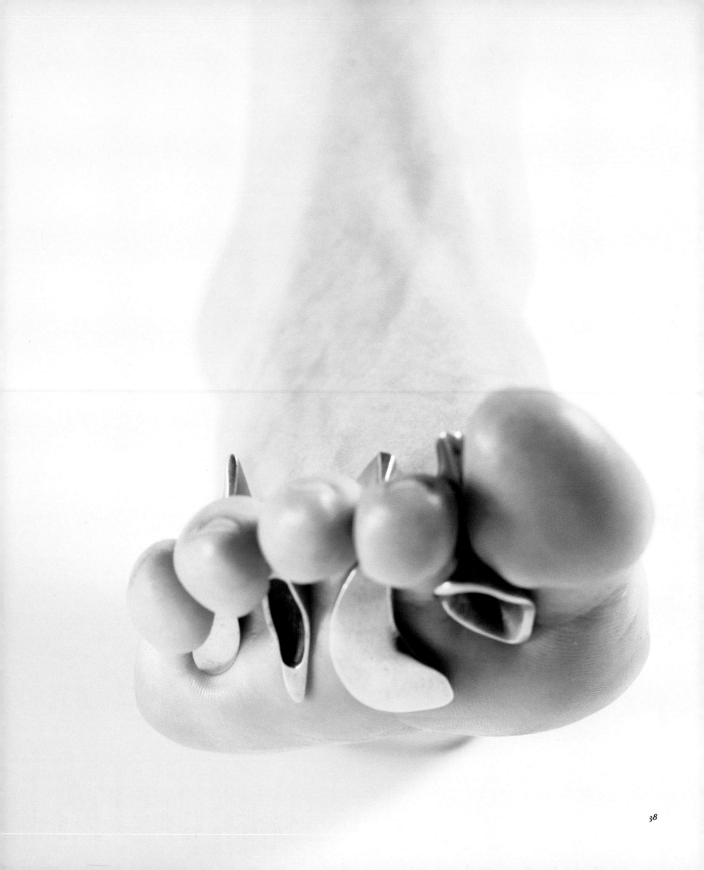

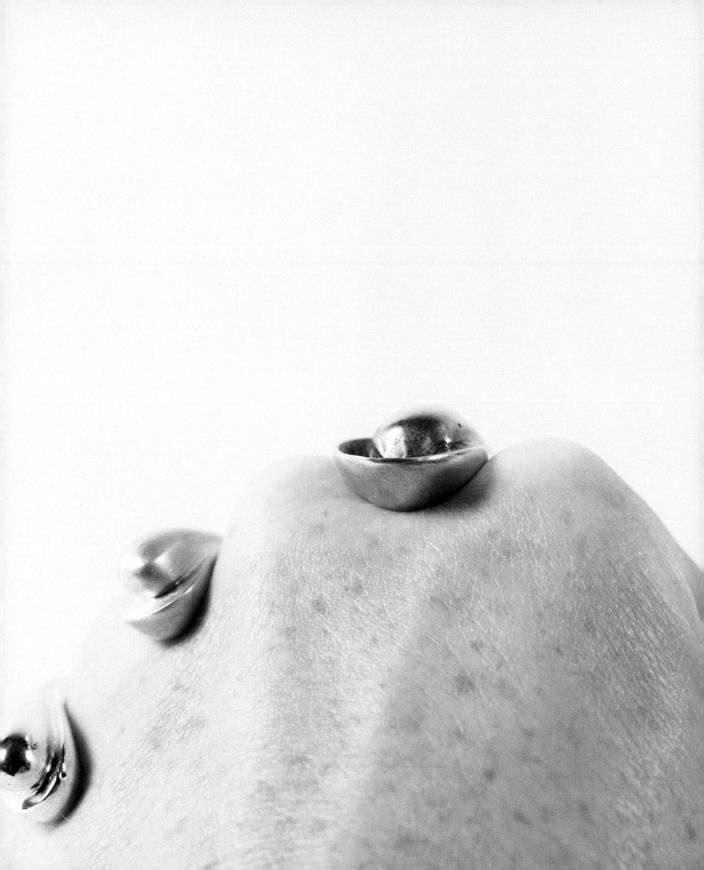

Mike *Turner*

Lars *Sture*

Shaun *leane*

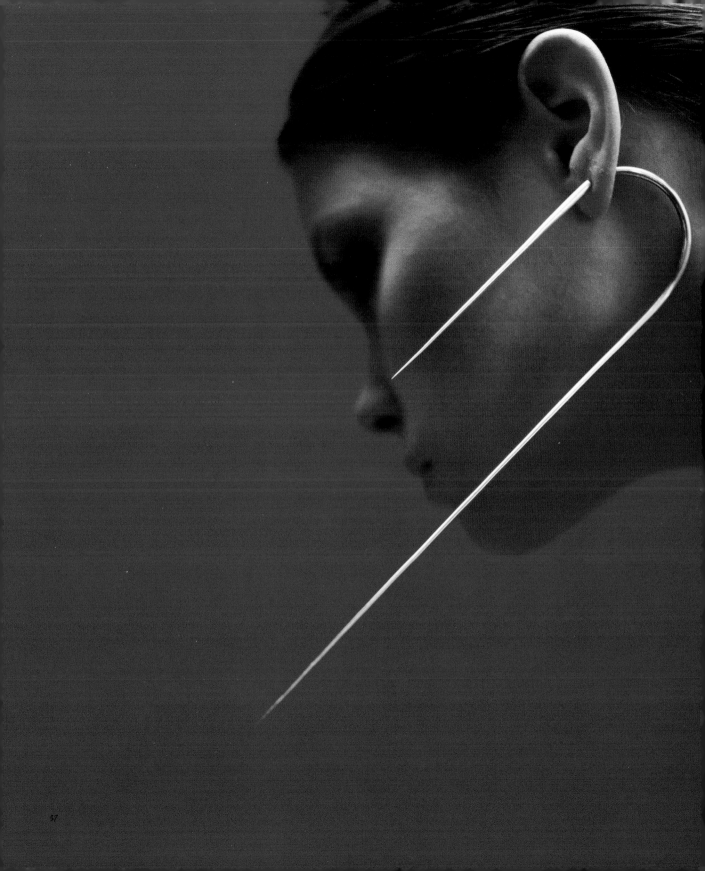

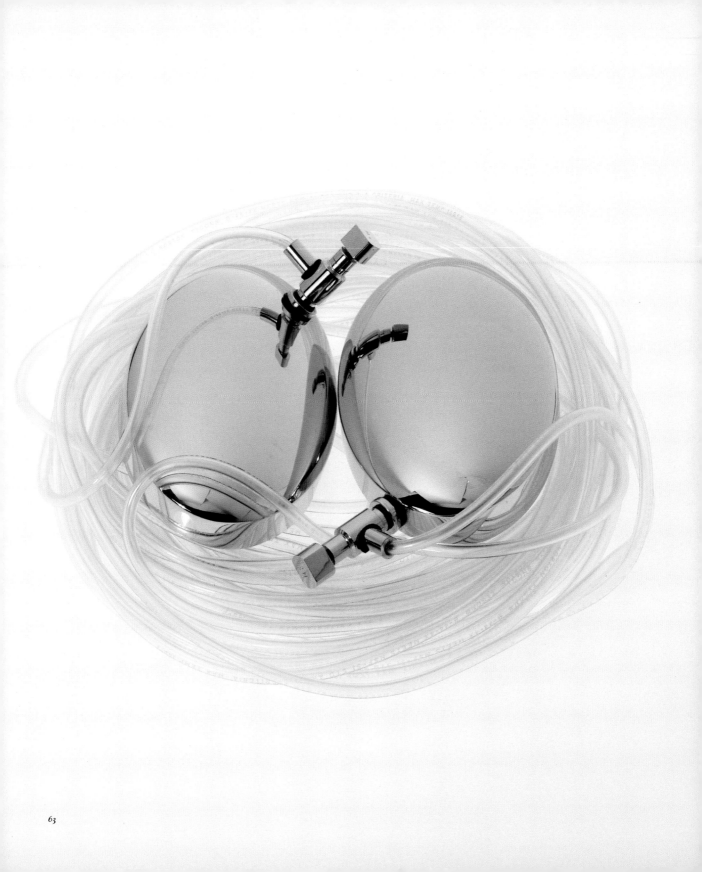

Erickson Beamon

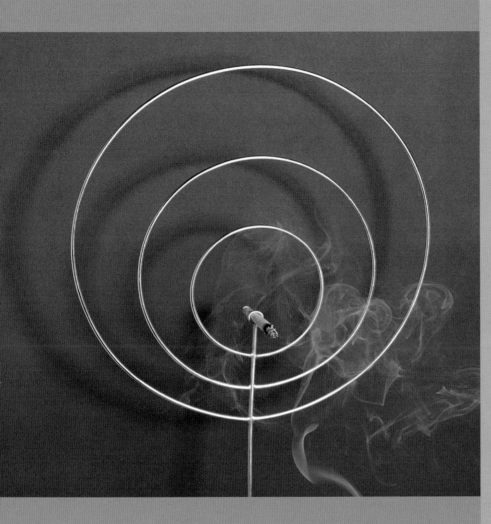

Lara *Bohinc*

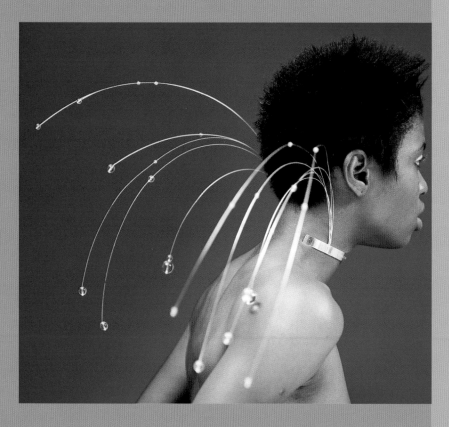

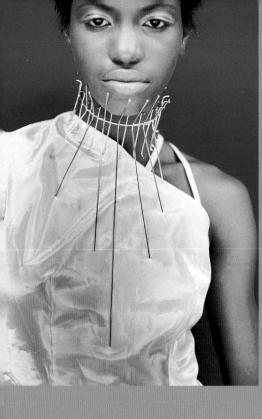

Nicole
Gratiot Stöber

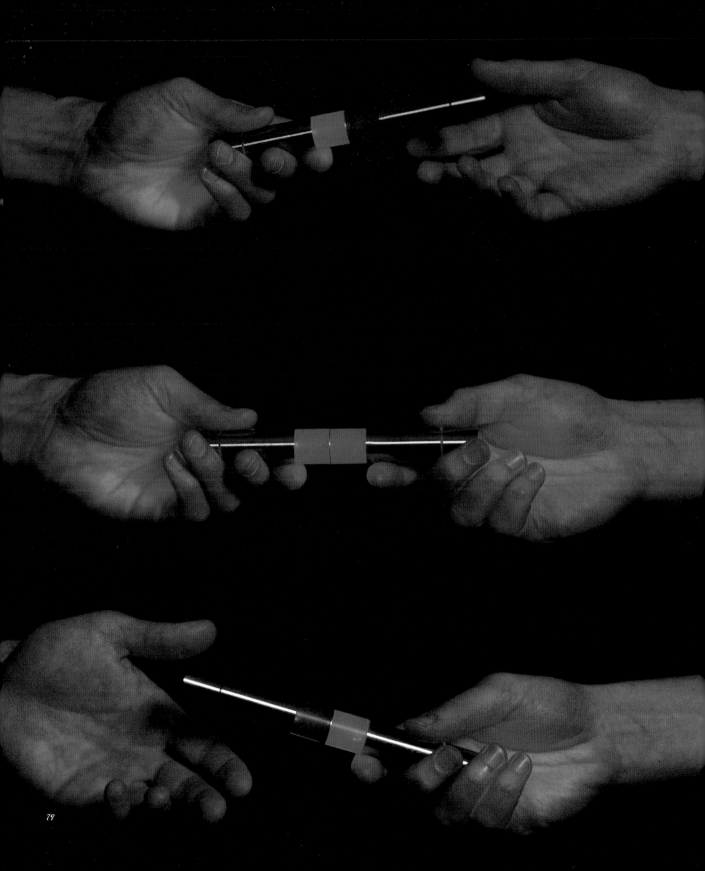

Sarah Harmarnee

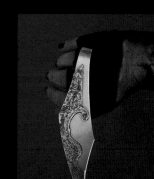

Mark Woods

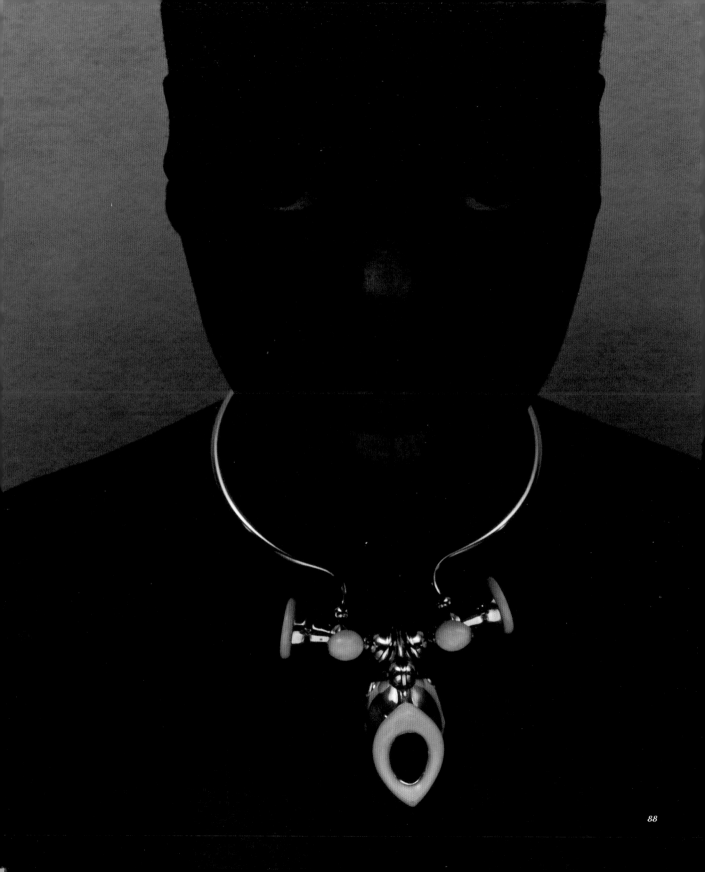

Laurent

Rivaud

Afterword

by Simon Costin

In some ways it is quite difficult to think about my work being included in a book about contemporary jewellery because so much has changed since I made it. The way that I worked and the processes involved were very different from that of many other contemporary designers at the time, as I was using materials which weren't readily associated with jewellery making. I tried to use these materials—such as fish skin, animal skulls and human fluids—with an intent which was more than just decorative. I liked the tension between people's reaction to the potential beauty of a piece and then their frequent revulsion at discovering that in fact the piece was 'real'. I was always interested in using natural objects, but in treating them as something beautiful and precious. I suppose this came from not having trained in jewellery or having had this sort of background—too often trained jewellers seem obsessed with technique instead of content.

It seems that much of the work included in this book has side-stepped these concerns and is far more aggressive than the work of the 1970s or 1980s. Contemporary fashion designers such as Alexander McQueen, have given jewellers the chance to explore areas within design that are difficult both commercially and conceptually. The jewellery featured in Alexander McQueen's catwalk shows—for example, the work of Shaun Leane, Dai Rees and Sarah Harmarnee—is both beautiful and seductive, yet also quite vicious. Shaun Leane's work is so 'sharp' that it could literally take your eye out and yet it is the vicious quality of his work that makes it sexy. Dai Rees' turkey quill head pieces, when seen on the catwalk, give the impression that the model's head has been skewered by day-glo spikes. Sarah Harmarnee's beautiful horn and silver pieces, using real animal parts, were made for McQueen's show, "It's a jungle out there", and perfectly complimented the savage aspect of this collection.

For me, it was vital that people seeing my work reacted to it strongly rather than just appreciating its odd beauty. I was very influenced by the turn-of-the-century Decadent writers and painters who used a mixture of morbid romanticism and hedonism to convey what were often quite extreme notions. I liked the idea that you could visually seduce someone only to have them repelled by the content or idea behind the piece. During this period, jewellery seemed to be the best way to present the ideas that I was interested in. Since then, my work has become increasingly unwearable. The last object that I made that could loosely be called 'jewellery', was a necklace comprising of a band of sprung steel overlaid with a large motor attached. Once on, it took ten minutes to constrict and crush the wearer. This was, I suppose, my farewell to jewellery.

There is both a mixture of beauty and horror in the work in this book. This jewellery has an 'edge' which is important at a time when commercial jewellery seems to have lost much of its power—for example, nobody even notices body piercing now, as its role in society has become extremely dull and predictable. People seem to be so visually jaded, so the idea of being moved by a piece of jewellery is pretty remote. Despite this, the designs here manage to be both beautiful and seductive and to catch you off-guard.

Erik Halley

b. 1971, France
Studied: ESMOD, Paris
Commissions: Julien McDonald,
Alexander McQueen, Jeremy Scott,
Erickson Beamon

Simon Costin

b. 1964, England
Studied: Wimbledon College of Art
Artist and jeweller.
Commissions: Alexander McQueen,
Sally Potter's *Orlando*, Derek Jarman's
Carravaggio

Scott Wilson

b. 1966, England
Studied: Royal College of Art, London
and Middlesex University
Freelance Jewellery designer
Commissions: Thierry Mugler,
Hussein Chalayan, Antonio Berardi,
Julien McDonald, Pearce Fionda and
Karl Largerfeld

Janice Taylor

b. New Zealand
Studied: Otago University,
New Zealand and
London Contemporary Dance School
Freelance jewellery designer
Commissions: Justin Oh and
Ally Capellino

Biographies

Naomi Filmer

b. 1969, England
Studied: Royal College of Art, London
and Wolverhampton Polytechnic
Freelance Jewellery designer
Commissions: Hussein Chalayan

Dai Rees

b. 1961, Wales
Studied: Royal College of Art, London
and Central St. Martins College of Art,
London
Freelance Jewellery designer
Commissions: Alexander McQueen and
Alexander McQueen at Givenchy.

Lars Sture

b. 1961 Norway
Studied: National College of Art and
Design, Oslo
Freelance Jewellery designer
Collections: Fabio Piras,
Joe Casley-Hayford, Owen Gaster,
Commune

Mike Turner

b. 1969, England
Studied: Middlesex University
Freelance Jewellery designer

Shaun Leane

b. 1969, England
Freelance Jeweller designer
Commissions: Alexander McQueen

H₂ Design

Emma & Jane Hauldren
b. 1967, England
Studied: The Royal College of Art,
London and Manchester Polytechnic
Selected Exhibitions: "Objects of Our
Time", Crafts Council, London
November 1996, "Jewellery, Past,
Present and Future", Galerie Ra,
Amsterdam, The Netherlands 1996

Erickson Beamon

Director of London branch—
Vicki Sarge
Jewellery collective based in London
and New York, originated in New York
Commissions: Ghost, Anna Sui,
Dries Van Noten, John Galliano,
Christian Dior, Rifat Ozbek,
Alexander McQueen for Givenchy,
Bella Freud, Clements Ribeiro,
Anna Molinari, Philip Treacy

Lara Bohinc

b. 1972, Slovenia
Studied: Royal College of Art, London
Freelance Jewellery designer
Commissions: Pearce Fionda,
Michiko Koshino

Nicole Gratiot Stöber

b. 1969, Germany
Studied: Royal College of Art, London
and Goldschmiedeschule, Pforzheim

Sarah Harmarnee

b. 1970, England
Studied: Victoria College of the Arts,
Melbourne
Commissions: Alexander McQueen,
Alexander McQueen for Givenchy

Mark Woods

b. 1961, England
Freelance Jewellery designer

Laurent Rivaud

b. 1968, France
Studied: Studio Bercot, Paris
Jewellery designer for
Vivienne Westwood
Commissions: Chloë, Givenchy,
Thierry Mugler

Erik Halley

p. 18. Silver ring with dyed red duck feather bone, 1997
Photo: Gavin Fernandes

p. 19. Black brass and porcupine quill choker over dyed in red, 1997
Photo: Gavin Fernandes

p. 20 left. Long Black Spider necklace – Haematite fire-polished beads and casoar feathers, 1995
Photo: Gavin Fernandes

p. 20 right. Cock and black turkey feathers earring and hair pieces with glitter detail, 1997
Photo: Andra Nelki

p. 21 top. Mother of pearl and 'pampille de coq' choker, 1995
Photo: Gavin Fernandes

p. 21 bottom. Double row beaded choker in topaz, aidue marine and orange collet light beads with 'pampille de coq', 1994
Photo: Gavin Fernandes

Janice Taylor

I initially started working in clear perspex as I liked that spacey look and contemporary feel. A lot of the fabric I use now comes from the unusable bits discarded by industry, so it promotes recycling. I really wanted to make pieces that were quite three-dimensional. If you make these shapes in solid colour it would be too much, so see-through perspex works well. I use quite cartoon-like shapes and cartoon colours to create a little bit of humour.

p. 22. Blue perspex ear cuff and choker
Collection: Spring/Summer 1997
Flat perspex ring
Collection: Spring/Summer 1996
Perspex choker with silver chain
Collection: Autumn/Winter 1996/1997
Photo: Andra Nelki

p. 23. Multicoloured interlocking perspex cuffs
Collection: Spring/Summer 1995
Photo: Gavin Fernandes

p. 24. Clockwise: Mirror curve-over perspex knuckle ring, U-V live-edge red perspex ring, amber stand-up perspex ring and lime curve perspex knuckle ring
Collection: 1996/1997
Photo: Andra Nelki

p. 25. Cream perspex choker and cuff
Collection Autumn/Winter 1996/1997
Photo: Gavin Fernandes

Simon Costin

p. 26. Bleached rabbit skull with silver wire and moss agate, 1988
Photo: Andra Nelki

p. 27. Dr. Dee's Skull Pin – Rabbit bones, copper, shell, horn and rock crystal, 1987
Photo: Andra Nelki

p. 28 left. Dried bream fish head – 18ct gold pin with haematite eye, 1986
Photo: Andra Nelki

p. 28 right. Claw Pin – Cold enamelled chicken's foot with graphite finish, haematite and rhinestones, 1988
Photo: Andra Nelki

p. 29. The Incubus Necklace – Copper, baroque pearls, silver, human sperm and glass, 1987
Photo: Andra Nelki

List of Illustrations

Scott Wilson

p. 30. Beaded eye patch –
Dyed perspex with crystal
Collection: Antonio Berardi
Spring/Summer 1997
Photo: Gavin Fernandes

p. 31. Horned mask crin shaped with
jet crystal beading, 1997
Photo: Gavin Fernandes

p. 32/33. Masks and veils – Flocked
spartrie shapes with draped chain and
jet fuchsia beading
Collection: Hussein Chalayan
Autumn/Winter 1997/1998
Photo: Gavin Fernandes

p. 34. Horned veil – Silver and silver
chain with jet and crystal beading,
1997
Photo: Gavin Fernandes

p. 35. Beaded eye band –
Dyed perspex with crystal beads
Collection: Antonio Berardi
Spring/Summer 1997
Photo: Gavin Fernandes

Naomi Filmer

I'm not a jeweller, I'm a jewellery
designer—I don't want to be
preoccupied by the traditions of
jewellery.

p. 36. Mouth Bar – Solid silver
Collection: Hussein Chalayan
Spring/Summer 1996
Photo: Gavin Fernandes

p. 37. Hand Manipulation Piece –
Cast silver, 1993
Photo: Andra Nelki

p. 38. Toe Betweens – Cast bronze,
1993
Photo: Andra Nelki

My work is not about what goes on
the body, but about the body itself.

p. 39. Finger Betweens – Cast silver,
1993
Photo: Andra Nelki

p. 40 left. Finger Between –
Cast silver, 1993

The light in the mouth is another
version of adorning the negative
space. Rather than wearing
something in it or on it, you expose it
and light it up.

p. 40 right. Mouth Light –
Resin casting, red LED lights and
single cell battery
Collection: Hussein Chalayan
Spring/Summer 1996
Photo: Gavin Fernandes

p. 41 left. Finger Between –
Cast silver, 1993

p. 41 right. Ear to Mouth Piece –
Cast silver
Collection: Hussein Chalayan
Spring/Summer 1995
Photo: Gavin Fernandes

Dai Rees

p. 42 top. Dressed black feather head
piece with flocked pelican quill
Collection: Autumn/Winter 1997/1998
Photo: Gavin Fernandes

p. 42 bottom. Yellow flocked feather
quill head piece with black dressed
feathers
Collection: Autumn/Winter 1997/1998
Photo: Gavin Fernandes

p. 43. Denuded feather quill head
piece with glitter dust and black and
gold gilded feathers
Collection: Autumn/Winter 1997/1998
Photo: Gavin Fernandes

I tried to set myself a brief of putting
a material together like a feather quill
and using it in a different way,
changing an object from one thing
into another. I strip feather quills to
make them look like something metal,
giving an impression of something
which is really heavy but is in effect
extremely light.

p. 44 top. Studded diamante neck
piece with denuded feather quill
Collection: Autumn/Winter 1997/1998
Photo: Gavin Fernandes

p. 44 bottom. Quilled constructed
head piece
Spring/Summer 1997
Photo: Gavin Fernandes

These pieces are not fantasy, they're
reality. When you wear one of these
pieces you have to be aware of your
environment, of who you are with, and
of how you can change that
environment by a simple movement. It
gives women a presence where they
are in control of their own environment
to a certain extent.

p. 45. Detail of quilled constructed
head piece
Spring/Summer 1997
Photo: Gavin Fernandes

Mike Turner

p. 46. Earrings, nose ring and lebrett –
sterling silver, 1997
Necklace – Etched copper and silver
plate with distressed rope, 1995
Photo: Gavin Fernandes

p. 47. Selection of lebretts – sterling
silver, 1996/1997
Embryo ear plug – Perspex, polyester
resin with sterling silver, 1997
Photo: Andra Nelki

p. 48 top. Finger extension – Etched
copper, brass and silver, 1995
bottom. Earring – Copper, brass and
silver, 1997
Photo: Andra Nelki

p. 49. Selection of hair pieces – Etched
copper and silver plate, 1994-1997
Photo: Gavin Fernandes

I work with electroformed copper and
cast glass. I used to love fossils. As a
kid, I collected fossils so it's obviously
had an influence on my work. I'm
trying to get a 'dug-up' feel similar to
ancient treasure when it has corroded.

These false human teeth are from
India. I have a strange fascination with
them and I'm not quite sure why I like
them. It is a vaguely 'tribal' thing in
the sense that since I started making
things, I've always liked the idea of
teeth necklaces, initially lion teeth and
that kind of thing.

p. 50. Pendant – Brass, copper and
sterling silver with plastic embryo
embedded in perspex polyester resin
with sterling silver, 1997
Photo: Andra Nelki

p. 51. Selection of bangles –
Electroformed copper, silver plate and
cast glass, 1993
Etched copper, silver plate and false
human teeth, 1995
Photo: Andra Nelki

Lars Sture

p. 52. Sterling silver pendant embedded
with human hair, 1996
Photo: Gavin Fernandes

p. 53. Patinated brass and human hair
necklace, 1996
Photo: Gavin Fernandes

p. 54. Sterling silver spiked knuckle-
duster
Collection: Fabio Piras Autumn/Winter
1995/1996
Photo: Gavin Fernandes

p. 55 top. Sterling silver chain
knuckle-duster
Collection: Fabio Piras Autumn/Winter
1995/1996
Photo: Gavin Fernandes

p. 55 bottom. Sterling silver zig zag
choker, 1996
Photos: Gavin Fernandes

Shaun Leane

My work is really minimal and often
very sharp. With this collection that I
did for Alexander McQueen, we
wanted as fine and sharp things as
possible to catch the light. There was
a line of light following the model.

p. 56. Speared choker – Sterling silver
Collection: Alexander McQueen
Spring/Summer 1997
Photo: Gavin Fernandes

p. 57. Speared earring – Sterling silver
Collection: Alexander McQueen
Spring/Summer 1997
Photo: Gavin Fernandes

p. 58. Silver face thorn – Sterling silver
Collection: Alexander McQueen
Autumn/Winter 1996/1997
Photo: Gavin Fernandes

p. 59. Tusk earring – Sterling silver
Collection: Alexander McQueen
Spring/Summer 1996
Photo: Gavin Fernandes

p. 60. Gem set silver halo –
Sterling silver and cubic zircon
Collection: Alexander McQueen
Spring/Summer 1997
Photo: Gavin Fernandes

p. 61. Silver mouth piece –
Sterling silver
Collection: Alexander McQueen
Spring/Summer 1996
Photo: Gavin Fernandes

H₂ Design

One of our main concerns is that the work is designed for young people. We find out new products and things which are happening at the moment and we base the designs and work around them, making new products in the process. We like conceptualising about the future and what's going to happen, but we actually think it's important to find out about new products and to push them a bit further—like the life-extension pill ring—which is both fantasy and fact. It's not just made up and that's the point. The function of the life extension pill replaces the diamond—it will be the idea of immortality for the future.

p. 62. Life Extension Pill Rings – Silver and steel, 1994

p. 63. Related Flask 1 and 2 – Chrome, brass, copper, tin and plastic, 1996

p. 64 left. Stomach Flask – Silver, 1994

p. 64 right. The Kiss – Silver and perspex, 1994

p. 65 left. Essential Underground Kit – Silver, neoprene and silicon, 1995

Our work is about designing for the new millennium with particular interest in the millennial preoccupations of genetic engineering, environmental change, urban club culture and virtual reality. Within these realms, the work transforms concepts for future eating and drinking. Each piece relates to the mouth and the flow of liquid from a container into the body. The work lies somewhere between science fiction, surrealism and futuristic fashion. Our influences have evolved from the revolutions in technology, chemistry and science. In this context working with computer technology for the first time on a project is a logical and apt progression for our work.

p. 65 right. Double Flask – 18ct gold plate, silver and rubber, 1996

p. 66/67. Saudade – Virtual reality head set – Chrome, brass, VR glasses, plastic and flock, 1997

Erickson Beamon

p. 68. Crystal, black diamond and comet argent light fire-polished beaded halter neck top
Collection: Ghost 1996
Photo: Gavin Fernandes

p. 69. Cyan and red crystal veil
Collection: Philip Treacy
Autumn/Winter 1997/1998
Photo: Gavin Fernandes

p. 70. Fuchsia and hyacinth crystal rhinestone head piece
Collection: Dries Van Noten
Spring/Summer 1997
Photo: Gavin Fernandes

p. 71. Haemetite and black diamond crystal balaclava
Collection: Philip Treacy
Autumn/Winter 1997/1998
Photo: Gavin Fernandes

Lara Bohinc

p. 72. Gold-plated steel cigarette holder, 1997
Photo: Andra Nelki

p. 73. Gold-plated steel wave choker, 1997
Photo: Gavin Fernandes

p. 74 top. 'Things Going on Around Me Seem Unreal' — Silver plated brass choker with text and glass beads, 1997
Photo: Gavin Fernandes

p. 75 bottom. Stainless steel wire and crystal beaded veil, 1997
Photo: Gavin Fernandes

p. 75 left. Chrome plated steel necklace
Collection: Pearce Fionda
Autumn/Winter 1997/1998

p. 75 right. Gold-plated steel and plastic headphones
Collection: Roger Lee
Graduate Collection
Royal College of Art, 1996

Nicole Gratiot Stöber

My work with light invites reaction. If the light is directed, it may appear decorative as well as personal, or even indiscreet. Light itself can therefore underline or replace the personal touch.

p. 76. Hand object — Wood, felt, steel, brass, perspex and touch sensitive electronics with light source, 1994
Photo: Andra Nelki

Each one of these responds slowly to touch, as though they require attention to come to life. After being held for a short time, these will slowly go brighter and brighter, then dim when released.

p. 77. Two Rings — 18ct gold, silver, perspex and touch sensitive electronics with light source, 1994
Photo: Andra Nelki

p. 78. Neck piece — Gold plated silver rose thorns, brass, perspex and touch sensitive electronics with light source, 1994
Photo: Andra Nelki

p. 79. Light Brooches — Stainless steel, nylon, magnetic clip and touch sensitive electronics with light source, 1994
Photo: Andra Nelki

Sarah Harmarnee

p. 80. Horn elbow piece — Hinged photo-etched silver plates with central horn and leather arm band
Collection: Alexander McQueen
Autumn/Winter 1997/1998
Photo: Gavin Fernandes

p. 81. Finger horn — Silver finger sheath with horn extension
Collection Alexander McQueen
Autumn/Winter 1997/1998
Photo: Andra Nelki

p. 82. Knife head piece — Silver-plated brass with photo-etched lace detail
Collection: Alexander McQueen
Autumn/Winter 1997/1998
Photo: Gavin Fernandes

A lot of my work is very inspired by equestrian tack. I love horses, their elegance and grace. The whole mood of the horse—the fragility and the strength, the poetry and the rawness. All my constructions have these equestrian elements to them, in the buckles and the forms.

p. 83 top. Blade neck piece — Sterling silver and human hair, 1996
Photo: Gavin Fernandes

p. 83 bottom. Blade knuckle duster — Silver-plated brass with photo-etched detailing and fingerless leather glove
Collection: Alexander McQueen
Autumn/Winter 1997/1998
Photo: Gavin Fernandes

Mark Woods

p. 84. Rosary — Hollow form silver, phenolic plastic, amber and 18ct gold, 1994
Photo: Andra Nelki

p. 85. Clamped — Sterling silver, 1996
Photo: Gavin Fernandes

p. 86 top. Hoover Head — Hollow form silver and phenolic plastic, 1994
bottom. Slanty Eyeball — Hollow form silver and phenolic plastic, 1997
Photo: Andra Nelki

p. 87. Spotty Wobbler — Hollow form silver and phenolic plastic, 1996
Photo: Andra Nelki

p. 88. Hole No.1 — Hollow form silver and phenolic plastic, 1995/1996
Photo: Gavin Fernandes

p. 89. Hole No.2 — Hollow form silver and phenolic plastic, 1995/1996
Photo: Andra Nelki

Laurent Rivaud

p. 90. Coral and horse hair earring
Collection: Vivienne Westwood
Autumn/Winter 1996/1997

p. 91. Camel teeth, agate and coral choker
Collection: Vivienne Westwood
Spring/Summer 1997

p. 92. Jadeite, mother of pearl and amethyst choker
Collection: Vivienne Westwood
Spring/Summer 1997

p. 93. Cat's eye, feather, chain and beaded earring
Collection: Vivienne Westwood
Autumn/Winter 1996/1997

p. 94. Jadeite, mother of pearl and amethyst choker
Collection: Vivienne Westwood
Spring/Summer 1997

p. 95. Dice, card, feathers and bird feet earring
Collection: Vivienne Westwood
Autumn/Winter 1996/1997

Editors: Alexandra Bradley and Gavin Fernandes
Design: Maria Beddoes and Paul Khera
Production: Duncan McCorquodale
Still life photography: Andra Nelki
Fashion photography: Gavin Fernandes
assisted by Paul Harris
Fashion art direction: Gavin Fernandes
Stylist: Samson Saboye
Models: Aimee, Lacy, Lillie, Courtney Miller
and Ragga at Wild International
Angelique, Johnny H, Becky and
Claire Harman, Kayon and Mari at Manique
Miriam Dietrich at Matthews and Powell
Hair and Make-up: Caitlin J. Maxwell
Clothes: Bernstock and Spiers,
Hussein Chalayan, Julien Macdonald,
Alexander McQueen, Errol Peak,
People Corporation, Fabio Piras,
Lawrence Steele and Vivienne Westwood
Cover: Naomi Filmer, Ear to Mouth Piece

The editors of *Unclasped* would like to express our
acknowledgment of a generous donation by Daniel
Gratiot, husband of the late Nicole Gratiot Stöber
whose work appears in this book.

The publisher would like to thank Katherine Clark
for her contribution to the conception and
realisation of this book.

The editors would also like to thank the following
individuals and organisations for their support in
realising this project:

Sidone Barton, Laurent Bayard, Anthea Benton,
Jason Campbell, Dionne, Felix, Kate Fitzmaurice,
Sarah Gilfillan, Jen at Bookings, Louise Jones,
Tracy Le Marquand, Mandy Lennard, Milena
Mihic, Mike, Richard Moore, Muriel Poncet, Vicki
Sarge, Dave Stewart, Philip Treacy, Michael Udo,
Trino Verkade, Ellie Wakamatsu, Nathalie Walters
and Lee Williams.

Thanks also to Joe's Basement and Rapid Eye
Colour Laboratories for in kind support towards
the realisation of this publication.

Printed by PJ Reproductions in the
European Union
© 1997 Black Dog Publishing Limited,
authors and artists.
All opinions expressed in material contained
within this publication are those of the authors
and artists and not necessarily those of the
editors or publisher.

British Library Cataloging-in-Publication Data.
A catalogue record for this book is available from
The British Library.

Library of Congress Cataloging-in-Publication
Data: *Unclasped. Contemporary British Jewellery*

ISBN 1 901033 35 X

Colophon